D1384374

FESTIVALS OF INDIA

India Book Distributors (Bombay) Ltd.

Publisher : **MELROY DICKSON**
Photographer : **RUPINDER KHULLAR**
Text : **ASHARANI MATHUR**
Published by India Book Distributors (Bombay) Ltd.,
1007 / 1008 Arcadia, 195 Nariman Point,
Bombay 400 021.
Tel. : 282 46 46/282 46 91/287 25 28/287 25 32.
Telex : 011-86085 IBD IN
Fax : 022-287 25 31

ISBN 81-7310-057-8

Printed at Thomson Press (India) Ltd.

FESTIVALS OF INDIA

ASHARANI MATHUR
RUPINDER KHULLAR

In India, the celebrations of fairs and festivals form a wondrous and joyful series of events, marking the rites of passage between birth, death and renewal. These moments are determined not by the pre-set dates of a linear calendar but by the changing luminosity of the sun as it enters new seasons, and in cycles spun out by the waxing and waning of the moon. Each full moon has its own meaning and is placed in the context of its own rituals, sacred or social : May, to commemorate the birth of Gautama the Buddha; July, to honour the guru or teacher; November, in remembrance of the birth of Guru Nanak, founder of the Sikh faith; October, to sip saffron milk in the mellowlight of the autumn harvest moon.

Along with the concept of consecrated time, there is also the concept of sacred space, one that goes beyond the immediate environs of temple, gurdwara, or mosque. The banks of a river, the meeting place of waters, a holy tank, forests, mountains, the seashore, the tomb of a beloved pir or saint.... all are areas of celebration and communion, where ritual prayers and blessings are followed by feasting, song and dance.

There are said to be more festivals in India than there are days of the year; not unlikely in a country where small, local village rituals of worship and propitiation are celebrated with as much fervour as are high holy days across the nation, occasions that can draw floods of people numbering half a million or more. Fairs and festivals are moments of remembrance and commemoration of the birthdays and great deeds of gods, goddesses, heroes, heroines, gurus, prophets and saints. They are times when people gather together, linked by ties of shared social and religious beliefs. Each of India's many religious groups – Hindus, Muslims, Christians, Sikhs, Buddhists, Jains, Parsis, and others – has its own such days. In a land of vast geographical distances and a variety of languages and traditions, the spirit and colour of these religious, seasonal or secular festivals underline the unity that draws together seemingly diverse groups.

But festivals are not new to India. This ancient tradition goes back to the Vedic times of the Aryans, and there are references to festivals to honour gods, rivers, trees, mountains, the coming of the monsoon, the end of winter, or the first flush of spring. The celebrations included not only fasting and prayers, but equally events of social and cultural significance. Performances of music, dance and drama took place side by side with more rugged physical activities : displays of valour and virility through chariot and boat races, or wrestling matches, and animal fights in which rams, wild bulls, elephants, oxen, horses and even rhinoceroses took part. Then, as always, there was much feasting and merriment to be enjoyed. There were *yajnas* (sacrificial fires), where milk, clarified butter and *somarasa* (the nectar of alcohol) were offered to the gods before being shared between worshippers. Special foods were cooked and served, prepared from freshly harvested crops. Elaborate garlands and ropes of flowers were woven as an offering to the gods and also to be worn over festive robes and jewellery. Such an assembly provided the opportunity to trade, buy and sell all manner of goods, from live-stock to silks, spices and handcrafted objects of ritual or everyday use.

Ancient Indians used to express these occasions through the words *samaja*, a gathering of people; *utsava*, a festival; and *yatra*, a pilgrimage or temple chariot procession. And though today we might use the word *mela* (meaning a fair) rather than *samaja*, it is astonishing how steadily and faithfully these traditions have endured over the centuries. Even today, *utsavas* or festivals are symbolic of a link between the home, the village, and a larger outside world. Within the home, celebrations are expressed by the love and care given to its decoration by the women of the house; freshly-washed courtyards are

embellished with designs made in flower petals, coloured powder or rice flour; walls are painted with scenes from the epics or made brilliant with embedded bits of mirrored glass; doorways are hung with auspicious mango leaves or marigold flowers. Each festival in each religion has its own particular foods and sweets, appropriate to the season and the crops, and days are spent in their careful preparation. In her home, the woman is an artisan in her own right, sharing with her daughters inherited family skills of garden and kitchen.

Outside the home, there is the brotherhood of community worship, moments when the barriers of caste and even creed are forgotten. There is the joy of the congregational *darshan* or view of the deity; the sharing of *amrit*, or nectar and *prasad*, or specially blessed food; the immersion of idols led in long, winding processions; the chanting of holy verses and partaking of the *barkat* or blessedness of an exemplary pir or saint. Festivals reinforce the presence of god in the life of the individual and the family, and bind them to the community. They are also moments for young people to absorb and be part of age-old, yet still vibrant and living traditions.

But festivals are also about fun and enjoyment, more so when they coincide with agricultural events such as harvests, a time to let go of the cares of daily life. The riotous exuberance and earthiness of Holi, the spring festival of colours, its almost Bacchanalian character, has the light-hearted atmosphere of a true Indian carnival.

Celebrations of festivals have their own special characteristics in different parts of India. If Mathura in northern India is famous for its uninhibited Holi and devout Janamashtami (the birth of Lord Krishna), then Calcutta is the city to see the Durga Puja, the ten-day worship of the great goddess who defeated the demon. Ganesh Chaturthi, dedicated to Ganesh, remover of obstacles, whose very

presence is auspicious, is best experienced in the state of Maharashtra. And nowhere outside of Kerala can you match the sheer spectacle of the caparisoned elephants of Trichur Puram or the snakeboat races of Onam. Differences of observance lend local colour to certain festivals – Dussehra, for example, famous equally in the south Indian city of Mysore, the Himalayan valley of Kulu and the holy city of Varanasi, whose celebrations in each place follow distinctly regional cultures.

The *mela* or fair can also be, and quite often is, connected to a religious festival or observance. The word comes from the Sanskrit root "mil," meaning meeting and mixing. In a *mela*, the mixing occurs on a truly grand scale; it is a meeting place for people from different villages, towns, and regions. The *mela* brings together a large variety of social groups : priests and mendicants; artisans and craftspeople; bards, jesters, dancers, musicians, and other itinerant performers; hawkers of fiery snack foods and iced drinks made of fruits and milk; vendors of toys, clothes and household merchandise; sellers of camels, horses or cattle, and families who throng from far and near.

The largest *melas* take place over a number of days, and often look like gigantic encampments, a multitude of small tents stretched out as far as the eye can see. As dusk falls, the lights of lanterns and cook fires sparkle in the gathering darkness, creating an air of romance and magic. And at some fairs, the ambience of romance is very real, for this is where the young gather to arrange their betrothals. At the Tarnetar *mela* in Gujarat, and the springtime Bhagoria of Jhabua district in Madhya Pradesh, young men and women wear their finest to the fair; and as they sing and dance together, shy glances and smiles often lead to marriage. "Come to Tarnetar," goes the traditional song, "for this is where you will find your loved one."

The *yatra* or pilgrimage is altogether more serious of purpose, and its intention is, as the name suggests, religious. In its most literal sense, a *yatra* can be undertaken at any time, for essentially it is the individual's journey to a specially holy place to meditate, pray for salvation, or as thanksgiving for a granted boon. In times gone by, devout pilgrims travelled for many months, often across vast distances and harsh terrain, to remote places like Mount Kailash and Manasarovar in the high Himalaya.

But *yatra* in its widest sense can be seen even today. On major occasions at the great pilgrimage sites, hundreds of thousands of people gather, drawn by the irresistible magnet of faith. The site of the *yatra* is sanctified by centuries–old tradition, and so many are centred around water – a holy river or its source, a sacred tank or lake, the confluence of waters. To immerse oneself in these pure waters is essential, for then one is cleansed of sin and renewed. The consecrated time is governed by the phases of the moon and sometimes – as in the Kumbh or Gomateshwara pilgrimages – can be as far apart as twelve years. Even annual pilgrimages draw vast crowds, as in the Rath Yatra of Orissa, where thousands of the devout join hands to pull on thick ropes, thus physically transporting the giant temple chariots on their journey across the town of Puri.

The terms *yatra, mela* and *utsava* are semantically correct and distinct. In real life, though, very rigid differences between these three occasions do not exist, and probably never did. Here, as everywhere in the world, solemn pilgrimages can also be fairs, and fairs can also be festivals. What is important is the meeting place of people, and the common language of shared human experience; the perception of the larger world as the larger family. And all three equally encourage this outward vision, a generosity of heart and mind, and indeed, is this not what celebration is all about? For in the end, all celebration is an exaltation and reaffirmation of life itself.

As the sun enters Capricorn, people in the Southern states of Tamil Nadu, Karnataka and Andhra Pradesh celebrate Pongal; their New Year, which coincides with the rice harvest. On the third day of Pongal, cattle are bathed, decorated, and fed the new rice (*opposite page*). Jallikuttu, a thrilling event where bulls are chased and caught, takes place at this time (*this page*).

The colourful Carnival in Goa takes place just before the austerities of Lent, and crowds collect to watch the merrymaking.

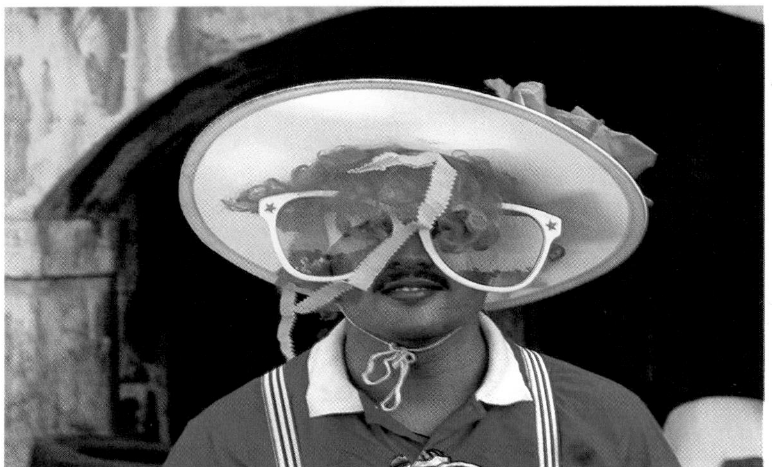

Momo is King of the Carnival, an occasion for music, revelry and a pageant of mobile floats.

Holi, the festival of colours, marks the end of winter, and is celebrated with great abandon in parts of Northern India. Coloured powders are on sale everywhere for family and friends to sprinkle on each other, either ceremonially or with great gusto (*this and following pages*).

Celebrated mainly in Rajasthan, Gangaur is the festival where women honour Gauri, or Parvati, the consort of Lord Shiva. Images of Gauri are worshipped, then carried in procession as musicians play or sing (*this page*), and the idols are immersed in a pond or lake (*opposite page*).

The harvest festival of Baisakhi is celebrated with verve, especially in the North Indian state of Punjab, where spontaneous joy is expressed through the Bhangra dance (*this page*). Important for Sikhs, Buddhists and Hindus alike, it is also marked by ritual bathing, as at Hardwar (*opposite page*).

The magnificent spectacle of Puram, a temple festival in Kerala, South India ... richly caparisoned elephants march in a stately procession accompanied by traditional musicians. Climax of Puram is the ritual exchange of parasols between two such processions and a dazzling fireworks display.

Ramzan is the most sacred and holy month of the Islamic calendar, a month of austere fasts. Then follows Ramzan Id, a time for celebrations, new clothes (*above*), and community prayers at the mosque (*left and following page)*.

Summer festivals at the Buddhist monasteries of Ladakh, such as this one at Thiksey, gather crowds of the faithful (*this page*). They feature ritual masked monastic dances to the accompaniment of chanting and traditional instruments (*following pages*).

Enthusiastic crowds in Bombay carry the image of Ganesh in a procession through the city en route to immersion.

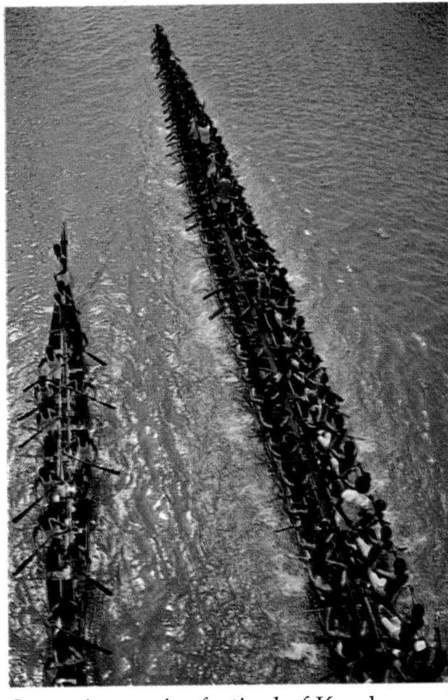

Onam is a major festival of Kerala, celebrated by all, and marked by floral decorations and festive foods. Palm fringed waterways form the backdrop for the famous snake boat races (*left page*), a special feature of Onam, as rivals surge towards victory (*above*).

Dussehra marks the victory of Lord Rama over the demon Ravana, of good over evil. It is celebrated differently in different parts of India. In the South Indian city of Mysore, it is a formal ceremonial sanctified by court tradition. The former Maharaja leads the festivities (*above*); and by night, brilliant illuminations outline the Palace (*left page*).

Two completely different processions : the pageantry of Mysore (*this page*) contrasts with a procession of deities in the Himalayan area of Kulu (*opposite page*).

Image of a Kulu deity carried in procession during the Dussehra festival.

Across the plains of North India, the climax of Dussehra comes with the burning of the ten-headed effigy of the demon Ravana over whom Lord Rama triumphed.

The period of Dussehra is observed in the Eastern Indian state of Bengal as Durga Puja, nine days of worship of the goddess Durga, commemorating her slaying of the evil Mahishasur. Each neighbourhood instals its own image of Durga (*opposite page*), where arati prayers are regularly performed (*this page*).

On the tenth day, the images of Durga are carried in procession and immersed in river, lake or sea (*this page*). In the same period, the Western state of Gujerat celebrates Navratri, literally, "nine nights", also in honour of the goddess. Women wear colourful clothes to dance the garba (*opposite page*), a joyful activity shared by the whole community.

Diwali, festival of lights, is perhaps the best loved and most universal celebration in India. Different legends are associated with its origin, but of major importance is the worship of Lakshmi, the goddess of wealth, invited into homes by the lighting of lamps (*opposite page*). Markets display clay idols for worship; and fireworks (*this page*), whose illuminations fill the night with radiance (*following page*).

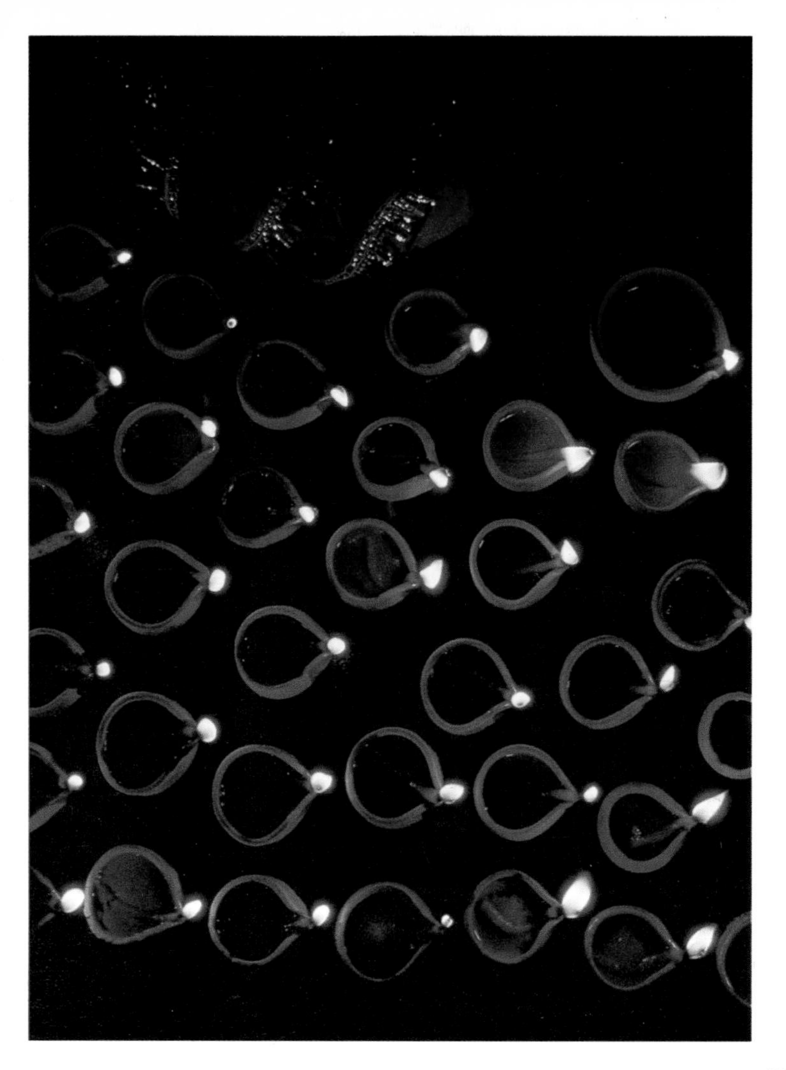

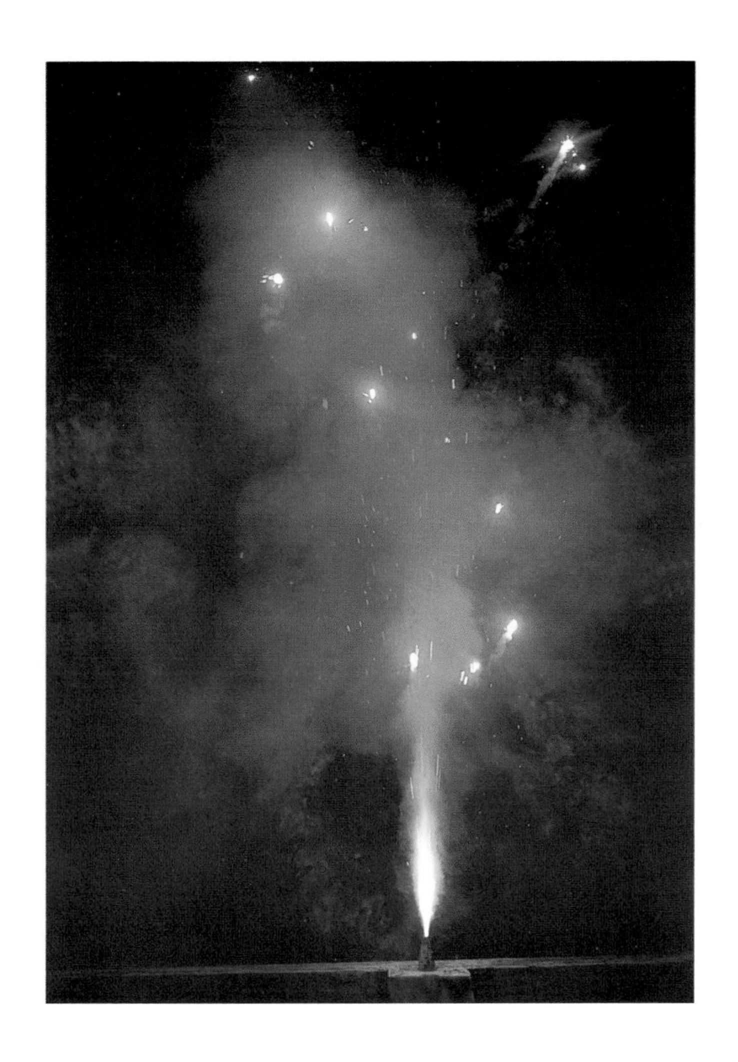

Celebrated mainly in Bihar, but also in Varanasi, Chhath centres around the worship of Surya, the sun, who is offered flowers and the holy waters of the Ganga. Temporary shrines are made of sugarcane stalks. Crowds throng the river bank for the ritual worship and bath or await their turn by the river.

One of the principal Guruparbs, or commemoration days of the Sikhs, is the day that marks the martyrdom of Guru Tegh Bahadur. Crowds gather at Gurdwaras to offer prayers in his honour (*this and opposite pages*).

YATRA / PILGRIMAGE

The Rath Yatra, which takes place in the temple town of Jagannath Puri in Orissa, Eastern India, is the ceremonial procession of huge chariots bearing the images of Lord Jagannath, his brother Balram and sister Subhadra. Hundreds of thousands of devotees join in to pull the chariots with stout ropes, forming a sea of humanity (*opposite page*).

SHOE STAND

Once in every 12 years is the Mahamastakabhishekh or ritual anointing of the giant monolithic statue of the Jain saint Gomateshwara. It is a sacred and significant occasion for Jain pilgrims, who throng by the thousands and watch or participate as an offering of milk, honey and butter is poured over the statue's head (*this page and following page*).

Though called Kumbh Mela, Kumbh is really a pilgrimage; moreover, that takes place in 12 year cycles at different places. Here, at Hardwar, lamps glow during evening prayers (*this page*). A surging sea of pilgrims awaits the ritual bath in the holy waters (*following page*).

At Baneshwar Fair, in Rajasthan, thousands of Bhil tribals gather at the junction of the Som and Mahi rivers in remembrance of their ancestors and for a holy dip (*opposite page*). As with all fairs, makeshift bazaars or haats spring up, where there is much buying and selling (*this page*).

Tarnetar, in Gujerat, is the scene of a huge three-day fair in August/September. For the Bharwads and Rabaris, tribals of the area, the fair is a romantic marriage mart, and folkdancing is an important feature. Young men gather in their traditional finery (*this page*), while crowds gather around the Shiva temple of Triniteshwar (*opposite page*).

One of the most colourful fairs in the country, Pushkar Mela in Rajasthan is also said to be the largest camel fair in the world, a giant encampment where hundreds of animals are traded each year.

But Pushkar is also a coming together of people, who, dressed in their finery, enjoy themselves. A dip in the sacred pool is a must.

Vivid colour, vibrant life ... this cluster of women at Pushkar seems to symbolise the spirit of the mela.